W9-ATI-829

INTRODUCTION

So no one understands your Japanese? Worse yet, you don't understand theirs. You've spent an entire week studying one phrase and you can't wait to use it. The big moment arrives—you're armed with the latest edition of *Learn Japanese in 27-and-a-$\frac{1}{2}$-Minutes-a-Day* for moral support—and you lay the phrase on some unsuspecting soul. What happens? The response isn't like the one in your book. Why? Basically, because the Japanese don't "play by the book" just as Americans don't "play by the book" when it comes to their daily language. So what to do? Well, you could quit and give up studying Japanese, or you could learn to speak real Japanese.

Just as we speak in a relaxed, colloquial manner, so do the Japanese. On the trains, at discos, during ball games, or in the company of friends, they all use shortcuts in their speech. If you want to speak the way the Japanese speak, then you need to know *what* to say, *how* to say it, and *when* to say it. Right? Okay, let's go!

INFORMATION

It's rather difficult to teach the correct pronunciation of a foreign language in a book, so we're not going to try. To help you though, we have arranged the words/phrases so that your pronunciation will approximate the correct, spoken form. We merged two and sometimes three or four words, or their derivatives, together, to create compound words/phrases. Almost every compound has been hyphenated in order to: highlight the union of merged words; emphasize the slang suffixes/particles and regular particles; and shorten the lengthy words to facilitate easier reading and memorization. *Fuzakenaideyo!* is a compound phrase meaning "Don't be stupid!" Its components are: *fuzake (fuzakeru)*, *nai (arimasen)* and *deyo* (slang suffix). The compound words/phrases were designed so you wouldn't pause during speech, but rather say the words in one breath. A pause in the pronunciation of *Fuzakenai-deyo!* would make the meaning less serious.

I'm sure you're familiar with the interrogative sentence forms of *desu ka?* and *-masu ka?* Well, these have gone bye-bye. Because of this dismissal, all words/phrases ending with a question mark should have the final syllables enunciated with a rising intonation, such as we do for "Right?"

9

To eliminate the embarrassing situation of using girl's words when speaking with the guys, or vice versa, we have denoted boy's words and girl's words with the symbols ♂ and ♀, respectively. A word/phrase denoted by ♂♀ can be used by both sexes. For example:

Nice to see you again.   *Mata atta-ne.* * ♀ (b→g)
                             Mata atta-na. ♂

   * Although *mata atta-ne* is a girl's phrase, the symbol (b→g) means a boy should use it when talking to a girl instead of the less polite *mata atta-na*.

Tomboy!   *Otoko onna!* * (b/g→g)
                             Otemba! * (b/g→g)

   * "Tomboy" is normally said only to girls, so these phrases are denoted by (b/g→g) meaning boy or girl to girl.

Is that so?   *Sō-nano?* ♂♀
                             Sō? ♂♀

Note: All words/phrases in this book are listed in order from most polite to least polite.

It seems to me that when a newborn Japanese baby is shown off for the first time, someone will say *Kawaii-nē?* (Isn't he/she cute?), and inevitably the whole flock of admirers will simultaneously say *Ne!* (Oh yes!). From such exposure the child is doomed to utter *ne* for the rest of his/her life. This is a bit fictitious, but the Japanese are quite fond of using the sentence particle *ne*.

There are two ways to say *ne:* the short *ne (ne)*—said with a falling intonation to show agreement or to add friendliness to speech; and the long *ne (nē)*—said with a rising intonation, often meaning "Isn't it?" or "Aren't you?", thus soliciting agreement.

Girls prefer *ne* and *nē*, so the guys must have a suitable alternative: *na* and *nā*. But if the guys wish to upgrade their speech, they should use *ne* and *nē*, especially when speaking to the opposite sex.

The meaning of some phrases may be changed from a statement to a question by changing *ne* to *nē*. These phrases are denoted by diamonds. For example:

| Haven't seen you around for awhile. | ♦ *Hisashiburi-ne.* ♀
♦ *Hisashiburi-dane.* ♂♀ |

can be changed to:

| Haven't seen you around for awhile, have I? | *Hisashiburi-nē ?* ♀
Hisashiburi-danē ? ♂♀ |

WHAT'S UP?

1

What's up?   *Nanka kawatta-koto atta?**♂♀

*Literally means "Has something special (unusual) happened to you?" Answers could be *Betsu-ni, Nani-mo* (both meaning "nothing much"), or a fuller description of whatever has happened. You can use this phrase in conjunction with *Genki datta?*, *Dō genki?*, or you can say *Dō, nanka kawatta-koto atta?* which means "Well, what's up?"

How's it going?   *Genki datta?* ♂♀
                              Dō genki? ♂♀

How are you?   *Genki?* ♂♀

How have you been doing?   *Dō-shiteta?* ♂♀

What's happening?   *Dō-shita?**[1]♂♀
                             Nanka atta-no?*[2]♂♀

*1. You know what's going on, but you missed a bit of it.
  2. You don't know what's going on.

What have you been doing?   *Nani yatteta-no?* ♂♀

What have you all been talking about?	*Nani hanashiteta-no?* ♂♀
Haven't seen you around for awhile.	◆ *Hisashiburi-ne.**♀ ◆ *Hisashiburi-dane.**♂♀

*The denotation of the diamonds allows these phrases to be changed from statements to questions. Changing the short *ne (ne)* to a long *ne (nē)* will cause the sentence "Haven't seen you around for awhile." to become "Haven't seen you around for awhile, have I?"

Is Sally okay?	*Sarī genki?**♂♀
How's Sally doing?	*Sarī dō-shiteru?**♂♀

*The answer to *Sarī genki?* will usually be "She's okay," and the answer to *Sarī dō-shiteru?* will usually be "She's okay. She has been doing . . ." or "She's okay. She went to . . ." *Dō-shiteru?* will solicit a longer answer.

Nothing much.	*Betsu-ni nani-mo.* ♂♀ *Betsu-ni.* ♂♀ *Nani-mo.* ♂♀
Nothing special.	*Betsu-ni kawannai.* ♂♀
Okay, I guess.	*Anmari.* ♂♀
I'm fine.	*Genki.* ♂♀ *Genki-yo.* ♀ *Genki-dayo.* ♂ ◆ *Māne.* ♂♀

What's wrong?

Dōka shita-no? *1♀ (b→g)
Dō-shita-no? ♀ (b→g)
Nanka atta-no? *2♂♀
Dō-shitan-dayo? ♂

*1 and 2 should be voiced with more concern.

What's on your mind?

Nani kangaeten-no? ♂♀

Nothing.

Betsu-ni. ♂♀
*Nan-demo nai-yo.** ♂♀

*_Nan-demo nai-yo_ is a response to "What's wrong?" or "What's on your mind?" _Nani-mo_ is a response to "What's up?" Don't confuse these two.

I was just thinking.

Kangae-goto shiteta. ♂♀

I was just daydreaming.	*Boketto shiteta.* ♂♀
Leave me alone!	*Hitori-ni shite!* ♂♀
	Hottoite! ♂♀
It's none of your business!	*Ii desho!* ♀
	Ii daro! ♂
	Kankei nai-desho! ♀
	Kankei nai-daro! ♂
	Yokei-na osewa! ♂♀

Colorful conversations can be created by injecting more than just a "yes" or "no." Study the following words/phrases. They can be voiced inquisitively or doubtfully, depending upon your tone of voice.

Really?	*Honto?* ♂♀
	Honto-ni? ♂♀
	Maji-de? ♂♀
	Maji? ♂♀
	Uso? ♂♀
	Uso-da? ♂♀

Is that so?	*Sō-nano?* ♂♀
	Sō? ♂♀
Did you? Do you? Are you?	*Sō-nano?* ♂♀

How come?	*Dō-shite?* ♂♀
	Dō-shite-dayo? ♂♀
Why?	*Nande?* ♂♀
What do you mean?	*Dō-iu imi?* ♂♀
Is something wrong/ different?	*Nani-ka chigau-no?* ♂♀
What's the difference?	*Nani-ga chigau-no?* ♂♀
What?	*Nani?* ♂♀
	E? ♂♀

Why not?	*Nande dame-nano?* ♂♀
	Nande dame-nan-dayo? ♂
Are you serious?	*Honki?* ♂♀
Are you sure?	*Honto-ni?* ♂♀
	Zettai? *♂♀

*Zettai? is a more emphatic way to ask: i.e. you really want to know if they are sure.

You don't mean it?	*Jōdan desho?* ♀
You're joking?	*Jōdan daro?* ♂

The following words/phrases will also liven up your conversation, or at least the speaker will think that you are listening.

That's right!	♦ *Sō-dane!* ♂♀
	♦ *Sō-dana!* ♂
	Māne! *♂♀

* *Māne* is often used to mean "I know." If said teasingly, it means "Yeah I know (but I might not tell you)."
EXAMPLE: "She's pretty, isn't she? Do you know her?"
　　　　　"Maybe I know her, maybe I don't." (*Māne*.)
Māne is also used in the jokingly conceited response "Yeah I know. Don't mention it."
EXAMPLE: "Your new car is bad!"
　　　　　"Yeah I know. Don't mention it." (*Māne*.)

Absolutely!	*Zettai-yo!* ♀
	Zettai-dayo! ♂

Definitely!	*Honto-ni sono-tōri!* ♂♀
	Honto-ni sō-yone! ♀
	Honto-ni sō-dayo-na! ♂
Of course!	*Atarimae-yo!* *[1]♀
	Atarimae-dayo! *[1]♂
	Mochiron! *[2]♂♀

* 1. Used in the sense of "That goes without saying!"
  2. Usually used as an answer to a question.

You better believe it!	*Honto-yo!* ♀
	Honto-dayo! ♂
That's it!	*Sore-yo!* ♀
	Sore-dayo! ♂
I guess so.	*Sō-dato omou.* ♂♀
	Sō-ja nai. ♂♀
It might be true.	◆ *Sō-kamo-ne.* ♂♀
	◆ *Honto-kamo-ne.* ♂♀

Maybe.	*Tabun-ne.* ♂♀ *Tabun-na.* ♂
Maybe not.	*Tabun dame.* ♂♀ *Chigaun-ja nai-no.* ♀ *Chigaun-ja nai.* ♂♀
I doubt it.	*Masaka.* ♂♀ *Uso-da.* ♂♀ *Uso-dayo.* ♂
That's not right.	*Sonna-koto nai-yo.* ♂♀
I wonder . . .	*Sō-kana . . .* ♂♀
I don't think so.	*Sō omowanai.* ♂♀
I'm not sure.	*Yoku wakaranai.* ♂♀

There's no way of knowing.	*Wakaru-wake nai-yo.* ♂♀

I can't say for sure.	*Nanto-mo ienai.* ♂♀ *Hakkiri ienai.* ♂♀
You're kidding me!	*Uso-bakkari!* *♂♀ *Uso-bakka!* *♂♀ *Uso-bakka iuna-yo!* *♂ *Uso-bakka ittenna-yo!* *1♂

* These phrases are commonly used by the Japanese, so don't confuse *bakka* (a short form of *bakkari* meaning "only" or "just") with *baka* (fool).
* 1. This is a bit harsher. It means "Don't be saying lies!"

This is too good to be true!	*Uso-mitai!* ♂♀
No way! (Stop joking!)	*Jōdan-ja nai-wayo!* ♀ *Jōdan-ja ne-yo!* ♂

That's not right!

Chigau-mon! ♂♀
Chigau-wayo! ♀
Chigau-yo! ♂

That's impossible!

Muri-yo! ♀
Muri-dayo! ♂
Dō-shiyo-mo nai-wayo! ♀
Dō-shiyo-mo nai-yo! ♂♀

Forget it! (I've had enough!)

Mō ii-yo! ♂♀

Bullshit!

Yoku iu-yo! *♂♀

* Literally means "How dare you say that!"

I don't care. (Anything's fine.)   *Dō-demo ii-yo.* ♂♀

It means nothing to me.   *Kankei nai-wa.* ♀
Kankei nai-yo. ♂

I'm not interested.   *Kyōmi nai-wa.* ♀
Kyōmi nai-yo. ♂

I think so too.   *Sō omou.* ♂♀
Sō-yo-ne. ♀
♦ *Sō-dayo-ne.* ♂♀

So am I. Me too.   *Watashi-mo sō.* ♀
Boku-mo sō. ♂

I see. (I got it.)   *A, sō-ka.* ♂♀
Sokka. ♂♀

All right, I understand.   *Wakatta.* ♂♀

All right, no problem.   *Ii-yo.* ♂♀

That was good.   ♦ *Yokatta-ne.* ♀
♦ *Yokatta-na.* ♂

Right on! (Great!)	*Yatta!* ♂♀
I did it!	*Ii-zo!* ♂
No problem!	*Rakushō-dayo!* ♂♀
It was no problem.	*Rakushō-datta.* ♂♀
Because . . .	*Datte . . .* *♂♀

* *Datte* is usually followed by an explanation.

But . . .	*Demo . . .* *♂♀

* Usually followed by a sentence or a short word/phrase, such as *Demo chigau-yo.*

GOT A MINUTE?

Got a minute?	*Jikan aru?* ♂♀ *Chotto ii?* ♂♀
'Till when?	*Itsu-made?* ♂♀
About when?	*Itsu-goro?* ♂♀
About what time?	*Nanji-goro?* ♂♀
Is it too early?	*Haya-sugiru?* ♂♀
Is it too late?	*Mō osoi?* ♂♀ *Oso-sugiru?* ♂♀
When is it convenient for you?	*Itsu-ga ii?* ♂♀ *Tsugō-wa?* ♂♀
How about the eigh- teenth?	*Jūhachinichi-wa?* ♂♀
Then when can you make it?	*Itsu-nara ii?** ♂♀

* You have already said *Itsu-ga ii?* or *Tsugō-wa?* and maybe even *Juhachinichi-wa?* and they still can't decide.

What time can I come over?	*Nanji-ni kureba ii?* ♂♀
What time do we leave?	*Nanji-ni iku?* ♂♀ *Nanji-ni deru?* ♂♀
What time do we arrive?	*Nanji-ni tsuku?* ♂♀
Are you ready?	*Yōi dekita?* ♂♀ *Mada?* ♂♀ *Ii?* ♂♀
When will you do it?	*Itsu suru?* ♂♀ *Itsu yaru-no?* ♂♀
How long will it take?	*Dono-gurai kakaru?* ♂♀
Maybe later.	♦ *Kondo-ne.* ♂♀ *Tabun kondo.* *1 ♂♀ ♦ *Sonouchi-ni-ne.* *2 ♂♀

* 1. You're undecided but you do want.
  2. You're undecided but you don't want.

Soon.	*Mō-sugu.* ♂♀
Not yet.	*Mada.* ♂♀
Not now.	*Ima-ja naku.* ♂♀
Last time.	*Kono mae.* ♂♀ *Konaida.* ♂♀

I don't know when.	*Itsu-daka wakaranai.* ♂♀
I don't know now.	*Ima chotto wakaranai.* ♂♀
I don't know yet.	*Mada chotto wakara-nai.* ♂♀
Someday.	*Itsu-ka.* ♂♀
Not next time.	*Kondo-ja naku.* ♂♀
Anytime is fine.	*Itsu-demo ii-yo.* ♂♀
Always.	*Itsumo.* ♂♀
You decide when.	*Itsu-ka kimete.* ♂♀ *Jā kimete.* ♂♀

That's a bad day for me.	*Sono hi dame.* ♂♀
That day is fine.	◆ *Jā sono hi-ne.* ♂♀

Let's begin!	*Hajime-yo!* ♂♀ *Jā yarō!* ♂♀
It won't take but a minute.	*Sugu-dakara.* ♂♀
Let's continue.	*Tsuzuke-yō!* ♂♀
Do it later.	*Ato-de shite.* ♂♀
I will finish soon.	*Sugu owaru.* ♂♀
I finished.	*Owatta.* ♂♀
Finished?	*Owatta?* ♂♀
Finished already?	*Mō owatta?* ♂♀

SAY WHAT?

3

Listen.	*Kiite.* ♂♀
Listen to me.	*Chotto kiite.* ♂♀ *Kiite-yo.* ♂♀
Don't listen. Don't ask me (that).	*Kikanai-de.* ♂♀ *Kikuna-yo.* ♂♀
Did you hear me?	*Kikoeta?* ♂♀
I couldn't hear.	*Kikoenakatta.* ♂♀
I didn't hear.	*Kikanakatta.* ♂♀
I don't want to hear.	*Kikitakunai.* ♂♀
Say something.	*Nanka itte.* ♂♀
What are you talking about?	*Nani itten-no?* ♂♀ *Nani itten-dayo?* ♂♀
You shouldn't say things like that.	*Sonna-koto icha-dame-yo.* ♀ *Sonna-koto icha-dame-dayo.* ♂

You said that, didn't you?

Sō itta-yone? ♂♀
Sō itta-desho? ♀
Sō itte-takke? *♂♀
Sō itteta-daro? ♂

* *Sō itte-takke?* means "I don't remember, but I think you said that, right?" It can also be used about yourself, such as "Oh, did I say that?"

I didn't say anything.

Nani-mo ittenai-yo. ♂♀
Nani-mo iwana-katta. *♂♀

* Should be used when a particular subject is in question, such as "Did you tell her my secret?" or "Did you spread the latest rumor?"

Let's talk in Japanese.

Nihongo hanasō. ♂♀

Let's continue to talk.

Hanashi-o tsuzuke-yō. ♂♀

Let's talk about it later.   *Sore-wa ato-de hanasō.* ♂♀

I don't want to talk.   *Hanashitakunai.* ♂♀

I don't want to talk about it.   *Mō sono-koto hanashita-kunai.* ♂♀

Don't make excuses.   *Iiwake shinai-de.* ♂♀
Iiwake yamete. ♂♀

That's not a good excuse.   *Sonna-no iiwake-ni naranai.* ♂♀

Stop complaining!   *Butsu butsu iwanai-de!* ♀
Butsu butsu iu-na! ♂
Monku bakkari iu-nayo! ♂

Do you know what you're saying?   *Nani itten-daka wakatten-no?* ♂♀

Don't talk so loudly.	*Sonna-ni ōkii-koe-de shaberanai-de.* ♂♀
Speak up.	*Motto ōkii-koe-de hana-shite.* ♂♀
Speak more slowly.	*Motto yukkuri itte.* ♂♀
Say it again.	*Mō ikkai itte.* ♂♀ *Mō ichido itte.* ♂♀

LOOKY! LOOKY!

4

Look!	*Mite!* ♂♀
Look at that!	*Are mite!* ♂♀
Take a look.	*Chotto mite.* ♂♀
Don't look!	*Minai-de!* ♂♀
	Miruna-yo! ♂♀
Did you see (it)?	*Mita?* ♂♀
I saw (it).	*Mita-wa.* ♀
	Mita. ♂♀
	Mita-yo. ♂♀
I didn't see (it).	*Minakatta.* ♂♀
I couldn't see (it).	*Mienakatta.* ♂♀
I don't want to see (it).	*Mitakunai.* ♂♀
Seen Jeff?	*Jeffu minakatta?* ♂♀
I want to see you soon.	*Sugu-ni aitai.* ♂♀

I saw/met Pablo.	*Paburo-ni atta.* ♂♀
So we've met again, eh.	*Mata atta-ne.* ♀ (b→g)
	Mata atta-na. ♂
I wanted to see you. I missed you.	*Aitakatta.* *♂♀

   * "I missed you" as in "I was lonely without you." Can also be used about a third person.

I'll show you.	*Misete ageru.* ♂♀
	Misete yaru. ♂
I won't show you.	*Misete agenai.* ♂♀
	Misete yaranai. ♂

TOUCH AND GO

5

Come here.	*Chotto kite.* ♂♀
Come over.	*Oide-yo.* ♂♀
Come later.	*Ato-de kite.* ♂♀
Can you come?	*Koreru?* ♂♀
Won't you come with us/ me?	*Issho-ni konai?* ♂♀
She is coming here.	*Kanojo kuru-yo.* ♂♀
I'm coming, wait a second.	*Ima iku.* ♂♀
I can go.	*Ikeru.* ♂♀
I think I can go.	*Ikeru-to omou-yo.* ♂♀
I can't go.	*Ikenai.* ♂♀
I want to go.	*Ikitai.* ♂♀
I want to go to Tokyo.	*Tōkyō-e ikitai.* ♂♀

I really want to go.	*Honto-ni ikitai.* ♂♀
I don't want to go.	*Ikitakunai.* ♂♀
I really don't want to go.	*Honto-ni ikitakunai.* ♂♀
You went, didn't you ?	*Itta-desho ?* ♀
	Itta-yo-nē ? ♀
	Itta-yo-nā ? ♂
	Itta-daro ? ♂
	Ittan-desho ? *♀
	Ittan-dayo-nē ? *♂♀
	Ittan-daro ? *♂

* These phrases are more positive, as in "I know you went because she told me!"

I went.	*Itta.* ♂♀
I didn't go.	*Ikanakatta.* ♂♀
Don't go.	*Ikanai-de.* ♂♀
	Ikuna-yo. ♂
Don't go yet.	*Mada ikanai-de.* ♂♀
	Mada ikuna-yo. ♂
I must go now.	*Ikanakucha.* ♂♀
May I go ?	*Itte-mo ii ?* ♂♀
Shall we go ?	*Iku ?* ♂♀

Let's go.	*Ikō.* ♂♀
	Sā ikō. ♂♀
	Mō ikō. *♂♀

* *Mō ikō* is said if you should leave because of the time, as in "We should go now or we'll be late."

Let's leave here.	*Mō deyō.* *♂♀

* Said only when inside a building, car, etc.

I'm leaving soon.	*Mō sugu deru.* ♂♀
She has left here.	*Kanojo kaechatta.* ♂♀
Stay here.	*Koko-ni ite.* ♂♀

Where are you going? *Doko iku-no?* ♂♀

Please go first. After you. *Osaki-ni dōzo.* ♂♀
Saki dōzo. ♂♀

Thanks for letting me go first. *Saki-ni gomen-ne.* ♀

Go slowly. *Yukkuri itte.* ♂♀

CHOWDOWN

I'm hungry.	*Onaka-ga suita.* ♂♀ *Hara hetta.* ♂♀
I'd like to eat something.	*Nanka tabetai.* ♂♀
I haven't eaten yet.	*Mada tabetenai.* ♂♀
Do you want to eat?	*Tabetai?* ♂♀
I don't want to eat.	*Tabetakunai.* ♂♀
I won't eat.	*Tabenai.* ♂♀
Did you eat (lunch/supper)?	*Gohan tabeta?* ♂♀ *Shokuji shita?* ♂♀
What would you like?	*Nani-ga hoshii?* ♂♀ *Nani-ga ii?* ♂♀
Do you want to eat some more?	*Motto taberu?* ♂♀
I'm thirsty.	*Nodo-ga kawaita.* ♂♀
I'd like to drink beer.	*Bīru-ga nomitai.* ♂♀

I don't want to drink.	*Nomitakunai.* ♂♀
I won't drink.	*Nomanai.* ♂♀
I haven't drunk yet.	*Mada nondenai.* ♂♀
Do you want to drink something?	*Nanka nomu?* ♂♀
Do you want to drink some more?	*Motto nomu?* ♂♀
Thank you, but I still have some.	*Arigatō, demo aru-kara.* ♂♀
Drink a little bit more.	*Mō-sukoshi non-de.* ♂♀ *Mō-chotto non-de.* ♂♀ *Mō-choi non-de.* ♂♀

Have you ordered?	*Chūmon shita?* ♂♀
How about (some) dinner?	*Shokuji shinai?* ♂♀
Is the meal ready?	*Shokuji dekita?* ♂♀ *Gohan mada?* ♂♀
It's ready.	*Dekita.* ♂♀
Will you try this (food)?	*Tabete miru?* ♂♀
(That) looks delicious.	*(Are) oishisō.* ♂♀
Smells good.	*Ii nioi.* ♂♀
Give me (some more).	*(Motto) chōdai.* ♂♀
Enough.	*Jūbun.* ♂♀ *Tariru.* ♂♀
Enough?	*Tarita?* ♂♀
Not enough.	*Tarinai.* ♂♀
I can't eat that.	*Sore taberarenai.* ♂♀
Is this delicious?	*Kore oishii?* ♂♀
It's not good.	*Yokunai.* ♂♀
It doesn't taste good.	*Oishikunai.* ♂♀

It's awful.	*Mazui.* ♂♀
What's that?	*Nani sore?* ♂♀
Not that.	*Sore-ja nakute.* ♂♀
What's it called?	*Nante iu-no?* ♂♀

I LIKE IT

7

I like it.	*Suki.* ♂♀ *Suki-yo.* ♀ *Suki-dayo.* ♂♀
I like it a lot.	*Daisuki.* ♂♀ *Daisuki-yo.* ♀ *Daisuki-dayo.* ♂♀
I hate it.	*Kirai.* ♂♀ *Kirai-yo.* ♀ *Kirai-dayo.* ♂♀
I hate it a lot.	*Daikirai.* ♂♀ *Daikirai-yo.* ♀ *Daikirai-dayo.* ♂♀
I don't like it very much.	*Anmari suki-ja nai.* *♂♀

* Someone is offering you something but you really don't want it. Say this if you don't want to hurt their feelings.

I really hate it.	*Honto-ni kirai.* ♂♀
I want . . . (noun)	*. . . -ga hoshii.* ♂♀

I don't want.	*Iranai.* *♂♀
	Ii. *♂♀
	Iya. *♂♀
	Yada. *♂♀
	Yada-yo. *♂♀

* The Japanese, in their sentence structuring, differentiate between wanting an object (noun) and wanting action (verb). If you want an object (for example, chewing gum), place the noun in front of *-ga hoshii*.

EXAMPLE: *Gamu-ga hoshii.* (I want gum.)

If you want action (to go), add *tai* to the verb (stem form).

EXAMPLE: *Ikitai.* (I want to go.)

Correspondingly, the negative form works the same way.

EXAMPLE: *Gamu-ga hoshikunai.* (I don't want gum.) Or you can just say *Iranai* (I don't want/need [it]); *Ikitakunai* (I don't want to go); or you can just say *Iya, Yada,* or *Yada-yo* (I don't want [to]).

Note: *Iya, yada,* and *yada-yo* are for action; *iranai* is for nouns; and *ii* is for either. And because these words are slang, they should not be said harshly, or their meaning would be too strong.

I really don't want/need (it).	*Honto-ni iranai.* ♂♀
I'm busy.	*Isogashii.* ♂♀

I'm happy.	*Ureshii.* (joyous) ♂♀ *Shiawase.* (fortunate) ♂♀
I'm happy to hear that.	*Sore-o kiite ureshii.* ♂♀
I'm glad to know that.	*Sore-o kiite yokatta.* ♂♀
I'm sad.	*Kanashii.* ♂♀
I'm fine.	*Genki.* ♂♀
I'm mad! I'm mad at you!	*Atama-ni-kichau!* *♀ *Atama-ni-kita!* *♂♀ *Atama-kita!* *♂♀

* For these phrases, *atama* is pronounced differently than when said by itself. These phrases should be said quickly and in a stepping manner, such as *ah-tah-mah-* . . . Usually these phrases are said jokingly; if I say to my wife that she's "silly," she'll definitely reply *Atama-kita!!*

I'm ready.	*Yōi dekita.* ♂♀
I'm tired.	*Tsukareta.* ♂♀
I freaked.	*Bibitta.* ♂♀
I'm surprised!	*Odoroita!* ♂♀ *Bikkuri shita!* ♂♀
I'm sleepy.	*Nemui.* ♂♀
I'm not sleepy.	*Nemukunai.* ♂♀
What a relief.	*Hotto shita.* ♂♀ *Yokatta.* ♂♀
I'm relieved (to hear that).	*Anshin shita.* ♂♀

I'm scared.	*Kowai.* ♂♀
I feel sick. (That's sickening.)	*Kimochi warui.* ♂♀

I'm disappointed.	*Gakkari shichatta.* ♀ *Gakkari shita-yo.* ♂
I was worried.	*Shimpai shita.* ♂♀
I can do it.	*Dekiru.* ♂♀
Can you do it?	*Dekiru?* ♂♀
I can't do it.	*Dekinai.* ♂♀
Can't you do it?	*Dekinai?* ♂♀
I can't help it. That can't be helped.	*Shikata nai-wa.* ♀ *Shikata nai-yo.* ♂♀ *Shō-ga nai-yo.* ♂♀
Sorry, I can't.	*Warui-kedo dame.* ♂♀ *Warui-kedo dame- da.* ♂♀
I should do it. I gotta do it.	*Shinakucha.* ♂♀ *Yaranakucha.* ♂♀
I'll do it.	*Watashi-ga suru.* ♀ *Watashi-ga yaru.* ♀ *Boku-ga suru.* ♂ *Boku-ga yaru.* ♂
I'm tired of it.	*Mō akite kichatta.* ♂♀ *Mō akita.* ♂♀
I understand.	*Wakatta.* ♂♀

I understand very well.	*Yoku wakatta.* ♂♀
I think I understand.	*Wakatta-to omou.* ♂♀
I don't understand.	*Wakaranai.* ♂♀
I don't understand very well.	*Yoku wakaranai.* ♂♀

I know.	*Wakatteru.* *♂♀
	Shitteru. *♂♀

* *Wakatteru,* which is used for action, means "Even if you didn't mention it, I knew that," or "Okay, I'll do it, so stop your nagging!"
EXAMPLE: "Go and clean your room." *Wakatteru.* (I know I need to do it.)
"The party starts at 7:00 p.m." *Wakatteru.* (I know [because I already heard about it].)
Shitteru can be used for nouns and actions.
EXAMPLE: "I know (her)" and "I know (how to get there)."
Shitteru.

I know that person.	*Ano hito shitteru.* ♂♀
Do you know that?	*Sore shitteru?* ♂♀
Ah, you know that.	*A, shitteru-no.* ♂♀
I don't know.	*Shiranai.* ♂♀
I didn't know.	*Shiranakatta.* ♂♀
I didn't know that, though.	*Shiranakatta-kedo.* ♂♀
You knew that, didn't you? You know that, don't you?	*Shitteru-desho?* ♀ *Shitteru-daro?* ♂
Give me time to think it over.	*Kangae-sasete.* ♂♀
I'll think about it.	*Kangae-toku-yo.* ♂♀

I'm so confused.	*Atama-ga kongaragatta.* ♂♀
	Nandaka yoku wakaranai. ♂♀
	Mō wakannai! ♂♀
I made a mistake.	*Machigaeta.* ♂♀
I blew it.	*Shippai shita.* ♂♀
Am I right?	*Atteru?* *♂♀
Am I wrong?	*Machigatteru?* *♂♀

* *Atteru?* and *Machigatteru?* are used to clarify whether or not what you've said or done was right.

Sample Conversation 1

Mike: She's late, isn't she? She said she would come here at eight o'clock, though.

Kanojo osoi-nā? *[1]♂
Hachiji-ni kuru-tte ittan-dakedo. ♂♀

Bill: I figured that.

Sō omotteta. ♂♀

Mike:	What do you mean?	*Dō-iu imi?* ♂♀
Bill:	I mean she won't come! I told you she's a playgirl, didn't I? She seemed like one. I knew I was right.	*Kanojo-wa konai-tte koto!* *Kanojo-wa asonderu-kotte ittaro?* *²♂ *Sō mieta-yo.* *³♂ *Sō-dato omotteta.* ♂♀

(It's past ten o'clock)

Bill:	See, I was right.	*Hora-na.* *⁴♂
Mike:	I can't believe it! That bitch! Let's go!	*Shinjirarenai!* ♂♀ *Ano ama!* ♂ *Deyō!* ♂♀

* 1. *Kanojo osoi-nē?* ♀
  2. *Kanojo-wa asonderu-ko-tte itta-desho?* ♀
  3. *Sō mieta-wa.* ♀
  4. *Hora-ne.* ♀

Sample Conversation 2

Sally: I'm so mad!

Atama-kita! ♂♀

Susan: What happened?

Dō-shita-no? ♂♀

Sally: The teacher said I cheated on the test. Can you believe it? I'm in trouble.

*Watashi-ga tesuto-de kanningu shita-tte sensei ga itta-no. *¹♀*
Shinjirareru? ♂♀
*Komatteru-no. *²♀*

Susan: I believe you. So don't worry about it. I have a good idea.

*Anata-o shinjiru-wa. *³♀*
Dakara, shimpai shinai-de. ♂♀
Ii-koto kangaeta. ♂♀

Sally: What is it?   *Nani?* ♂♀

(Silence)

Susan: Understand?   *Wakatta?* ♂♀
Okay, I'll help you.   *Jā, tetsudau-wa.* *[4]♀

Sally: You're a life saver.   *Tasukatta-wa.* *[5]♀
I know I can count   *Tayori-ni shiteru-wa.* *[6]♀
on you.

* 1. *Boku-ga tesuto-de kanningu shita-tte sensei-ga ittan-da.* ♂
  2. *Komatterun-da.* ♂
  3. *Shinjiru-yo.* ♂
  4. *Tetsudau-yo.* ♂
  5. *Tasukatta-yo.* ♂
  6. *Tayori-ni shiteru-yo.* ♂

Sample Conversation 3

Husband: How many (bags) can you carry?   *Ikutsu motte-ikeru?* ♂♀

Wife: Three.   *Mittsu.* ♂♀

Husband: Here you are.   *Hai-yo.* ♂♀

Wife: Wait a minute. I think I can take four. Give me another one.

Chotto matte. ♂♀
Yotsu motte-ikeru. ♂♀
Mō hitotsu chōdai. ♂♀

Husband: I don't think so. Isn't that too much?

Sō omowanai-kedo. ♂♀
Ō-sugi-nai? ♂♀

Wife: It's okay. Believe me.

Heiki. Shinjite. ♂♀

(She starts to stagger)

Wife: Help! Won't you help me?

Tasukete! ♂♀
Tetsudatte kurenai? ♂♀

Husband: Okay.
Now you see.
You're such a little girl.
I knew you couldn't make it.
I told you so!

Ii-yo. ♂♀
Sore miro. *[1]♂♀
Kimi-wa kayowain-dakara ♂
Dekinai-tte wakat-teta. ♂♀
Sō itta-daro! *[2]♂

* 1. *Hora, mina-yo.* ♂♀
  2. *Sō itta-desho!* ♀

BAD WORDS!

8

What do you want?!

Nani-yo?! ♀
Nanda-yo! ♂
*Nanka monku aru-no-
ka?* ♂

* Basic, all-around good phrases to use when someone really pisses you off. These phrases usually command respect, or at least they allow you to establish yourself.

Do you want to say something?!

Nanka yō?! ♂♀

* Japanese are infamous for staring. To have them return to their own affairs, a simple *Nanda-yo?!* or *Nanka yō?!* works well. But then again, the Japanese are known for their persistence, too. If these two fail, simply tell them:

Don't look at me!

Kochi minai-deyo! ♀
Kochi miruna-yo! ♂
Miten-ja nēyo! ♂

Don't stare at me!

Jiro jiro minai-deyo! ♀
Jiro jiro miruna-yo! ♀
*Gan tobashiten-ja
nēyo!* ♂

What did you say?	*Nante itta-noyo?* ♀ *Nante ittan-dayo?* ♂
Who do you think you're talking to?	*Dare-ni mukatte mono itten-dayo?* ♂
Why do you talk like that?!	*Nande sonna-koto iu-noyo?!* *♀ *Nande sonna-koto iun-dayo?!* *♂

* If you're positive a Japanese person is talking derogatorily about you, these phrases are good to use. But be careful; sometimes they're complimenting you!

You're stupid!	*Baka-ja nai!* ♀ *Baka!* ♂♀ *Tako!* ♂♀ *Baka-yarō!* ♂
You look stupid!	*Baka-mitai!* ♂♀

That's stupid!	*Baka-mitai!* ♂♀ *Baka-jan!* *♂♀

* *-jan* is a colloquial suffix coined in Yokohama. It is used with a variety of words, so keep your ears open.

What you did was stupid!	*Baka-da!* ♂♀
You're crazy!	*Kichigai!* ♂♀
Don't act stupid!	*Baka yamete-yo!* *♀ *Baka yamero-yo!* *♂ *Baka yamena-yo!* *♀ *Baka yatten-ja nēyo!* *♂ *Fuzakenai-deyo!* *♀ *Fuzakeruna-yo!* *♂ *Fuzaken-ja nēyo!* *♂

* These phrases can be used when someone pisses you off. They translate as "Don't joke around with me!" or "Don't think I am lower than you!" Phrases beginning with *baka* can also be voiced with concern for a friend's silly, irrational behavior.

Don't say stupid things!	*Baka iwanai-deyo!* ♀
	Baka ittenna-yo! ♂
	Netenna-yo! *♂

* *Netenna-yo!* means "Wake up!"

Liar!	*Usotsuki!* ♂♀

You've got a big mouth!	*Oshaberi!* *♂♀

* Always spreading the latest rumor, people's secrets, etc.

Get your head out of your ass!	*Neboken-ja nēyo!* *♂

* Literally means "Aren't you half-asleep (because of what you did/are doing)?" Depending upon your tone of voice, this phrase can be funny or very harsh.

That's a lie!	*Sonna-no uso-yo!* ♀
	Sonna-no uso-dayo! ♂
	Uso bakkari! ♂♀
	Fukashi-jan! ♂

Don't lie!	*Uso tsukanai-deyo!* ♀
	Uso tsukuna-yo! ♂
	Fukashi ittenna-yo! ♂

| Stop it! | *Yamete-yo!* ♀ |
| | *Yamero-yo!* ♂ |

| You shouldn't do that! | *Dame-yo!* ♀ |
| | *Dame-dayo!* ♂ |

| Why do you do something like that? | *Nande sonna-koto suru-no?* ♂♀ |

| Why did you do such a thing? | *Nande sonna-koto shita-no?* ♂♀ |

| Leave him/her alone! | *Hottoke-ba!* ♂♀ |
| | *Hottoke-yo!* ♂ |

| Do as I say! | *Itta-tōri-ni shite!* ♀ |
| | *Itta-tōri-ni shiro-yo!* ♂ |

| This is the limit! | *Ii kagen-ni shite-yo!* ♀ |
| | *Ii kagen-ni shiro-yo!* ♂ |

Stop it!	*Shitsukoi!* *♂♀

* When someone is being persistent.

Give it back!	*Kaeshite-kure!* ♂♀
	Kaeshite-yo! ♀
	Kaese-yo! ♂
Leave me alone!	*Hottoite-yo!* ♀
	Hottoite-kure-yo! ♂
Leave us alone!	*Watashitachi-dake-ni shite-yo!* ♀
	Bokutachi-dake-ni shite-kure-yo! ♂

Get out of here!	*Mukō-ni itte-yo!* ♀
	Achi itte-yo! ♀
	Achi ike-yo! ♂
	Dokka ichimē-yo! ♂
Come here!	*Chotto kochi kite!* ♀
	Kochi oide-yo! ♀ (b→g)
	Kochi koi-yo! ♂

You're noisy!	*Urusai-wane!* ♀ *Urusē-na!* ♂ *Urusē-yo!* ♂ *Urusēn-dayo!* ♂

Shut up!	*Damatte-yo!* ♀ *Damare-yo!* ♂
Stop your babbling!	*Gatagata itten-ja nēyo!* ♂
Be quiet!	*Shizuka-ni shite- yo!* *♀ (b→g) *Shizuka-ni shiro-yo!* *♂

* If in a movie theater, pub, etc., first you should say *Shizuka-ni shite kudasai.* If there are no results, *Shizuka-ni shite-yo!* or *Shizuka-ni shiro-yo!* should do the trick. Still no progress? Throw in a couple of *Urusēn-dayo!*'s. Both phrases can be used playfully between boyfriend and girlfriend.

You asshole!	*Kono kuso-ttare!* *♂

* Literally means ''You have shit around your asshole!''

You bitch!	*Kono ama!* (b/g→g)

You whore!   *Yariman!* *(b/g→g)

 * *Yariman!* means a girl who will go to bed with anyone.

Home boy!   *Kono imo!* *♂♀

 * Literally means "You potato!" Comes from the fact that potatoes are grown in the country. You can also say *imo nē-chan* and *imo nī-chan* to mean "potato girl" and "potato boy," respectively. You're saying they are unfashionable, or that their talk is uncool.

Playboy!   *Onna-tarashi!* *(g→b)

 * A bad word to say to boys.

Shorty!   *Chibi!* ♂♀
                                    Gaki! ♂♀

Short legs!   *Tansoku!* ♂♀

Weakling!   *Yowa-mushi!* ♂♀

You ain't got balls!   *Konjō nashi!* *♂♀

    * Means you're lacking in the "brave" department.

You're ugly!   *Busu!* (ugly girl) *(b/g→g)
                       Geso! (ugly boy) (g→b)

    * *Busu!* is the worst word to say to a girl.

You pig!   *Buta!* *♂♀
              Debu! *♂♀

    * Said to girls and to obese boys. Again, bad words to say to a girl.

Fag!   *Okama!** (b/g→b)

    * Said to a boy who acts or dresses in a feminine manner.

Tomboy!   *Otoko onna!* (b/g→g)
                Otemba! (b/g→g)

White boy!	*Haku-jin!* *♂♀
	Yankī! *♂♀
	Shiro! *♂♀
	Kimpatsu! *♂♀

* *Yankī!* and *Shiro!* are Japanese slurs for white people. *Yankī!*, which comes from "Yankee," is for Americans, and *Haku-jin!* and *Shiro!* are for all Caucasians. *Kimpatsu* means "blond hair."

You're the lowest!	*Saitei-yo!* ♀
	Saitei-dayo! ♂♀
You're narrow minded!	*Ketsu-no ana-no chīsai-yarō!* *♂

* Literally means "Your asshole is small!"

Don't be so cocky!	*Namaiki iun-ja naiyo!* ♂♀
You're a tightwad!	*Kechi!* ♂♀
	Do-kechi! ♂♀
You're a dirtbag!	*Kitanai!* ♂♀
Don't fuck with me!	*Namenna-yo!* *♂
	Namen-ja nēyo! *♂
	Nametenna-yo! *♂

* Literally means "Don't lick me!" A not-so-literal translation puts it as "Don't joke around with me!" or "Don't think I am lower than you!"—i.e. if someone says *Nandayo?* to you, just say one of the above and walk away (as the winner).

Get away! (Fuck off!)

Mukō itte-yo! ♀
Dokka itte-yo! ♀
Dokka ike-yo! ♂
Hayaku inakunare-yo! ♂
Hayaku kiena! ♂
Urochoro shittenna! ♂
Totto-to usero! ♂

If you don't have time to socialize, just say one or two of these "parting shots" as you walk away: *Baka-ja nai!* ♀ (You're stupid!); *Baka-mitai!* ♀ (You look stupid!); *Yanayatsu!* ♀ (What a nasty person!); *Henna-yatsu!* ♂ (What a geek!); *Henna-yarō!* ♂ (What a chump!); *Baka-ja nēno!* ♂ (Oh, how stupid!); *Baka-jan!* ♂ (That's so stupid!).

Fuck you!/Go to hell!

Kutabare! ♂
Shinjimae! ♂

Don't try to be cool!	*Tsuppaten-ja nēyo!* ♂
	Ikigatten-ja nēyo! ♂
Let's finish this now!	*Kerio tsuke-yōze!* ♂
I'm going to kick your ass!	*Bukkoroshite yaru!* *♂

* Literally means "I'm going to hit you till you die!" This is a harsh phrase: expect to throw a few punches after you say this one.

You dog!!	*Temē kono-yarō!!* *♂

* Serious fighting words! Usually said before or while the right hook is connecting.

Have you ever noticed that while you're waiting in line for something—it doesn't matter what—for some reason people seem to think *their* position is at the front of the line? The following phrases should get your point across.

We're making a line.	*Naranderun-dakedo.* ♂♀
Don't push!	*Osanai-deyo!* ♀
	Osuna-yo! ♂
That hurts!	*Itai-wane!* *♀
	Itē-na! *♂

* These phrases are said to ensure the offender knows you're hurt. *Itai* is said when you hurt yourself.

You little rat! (Check this geek out!)   *Nani koitsu!* *♂♀

> * Said about anyone doing anything, but usually not to their face.

Who do you think you are?!   *Nani-yo anta?!* *♀
Nani temē?! *♂

> * *Anta* is a shorter way for girls to say *anata* (you). In the *Kantō* area, *anta* is considered to be harsher than *anata*. *Temē* is a bad boy's word for "you." *Nani-yo anta?!* and *Nani temē?!* can be said to their face.

What's this old man doing?!   *Nani kono jijī?!* *♂♀
Nanda-yo kono jijī?! *♂♀

What's this old woman doing?!

Nani kono babā?! *♂♀
Nanda-yo kono babā?! *♂♀

* *Jijī* is from *ojī-san* (grandfather/old man) and *babā* is from *obā-san* (grandmother/old woman).

Damn it!

Chikusho! *♂♀

* Usually said to yourself.

Shit!

Unko! *♂♀
Kuso! *♂♀

* Both words mean "feces," but *Kuso!* can be said to yourself, such as Americans say "Shit!"

Shit, I fucked up! Oh, shit!	*Ikkenai!* *♀ *Ikkene!* *♂

* Literally means "It's not good!" Usually said to yourself.

Chikan is the Japanese word for a stranger who enjoys doing perverse sexual acts to young, sexy-looking girls. These strangers like to touch any part of the girl's body, put their body against the girl's body, and to "flash." The *chikan* usually rides the train during the morning and late afternoon rush hours to benefit from the proximity of the passengers. Most girls will freak-out during this experience and the few that don't might slap the offender and/or verbally accuse him of sexual harassment. The transgressor might counterattack by saying something like *Dare-ga omae-nanka sawarukayo?!* (Who would want to touch you?!). The sad part of this story is that no one will come to the rescue. The people on the train will pacifistically look away as if nothing happened. For the guy who would like to score a few "brownie points," give your assistance in a situation like this. Everyone will be suprised—probably even more surprised than the *chikan*. But, if Superman isn't around the corner, the only recourse is to use the following words/phrases and the others listed in this chapter.

Lewd! Vulgar!   *Sukebe!* *♀

Sexual perversion.   *Hentai.* *♂♀
  Abnormality.

> * Placing *kono* in front of *sukebe* and *hentai* will direct the
> attention to one person, such as *Kono sukebe!* (You freak!)
> and *Kono hentai!* (You pervert!).

Take your hand(s) off!   *Te-o dokete-yo!* ♀

Don't touch me!   *Sawannai-de!* ♀

If all else fails, try these phrases:

You're dirty!   *Kitanai-wane!* ♀

Your "tool" is small!   *Tansho!* ♀

A couple of years ago, Erika and I went to a discotheque in Tokyo. As I was preparing to pay the admission charge, I learned our fee was almost twice the norm! There was no doubt in my mind as to why, but I became so irate we just left. However, the second time this happened we settled the problem right away. If this happens to you, and you are determined to patronize the place (remember—it's the principle of the matter), the first thing you should do is let them know you speak and understand Japanese. That will definitely throw them off guard, thus reducing their likelihood of continuing the scheme. Say anything pertaining to the situation because they know what you're talking about. If they ask you questions, don't worry about answering them. Just keep stressing what you want. If they don't give in, do what you would do in America—call for the manager!

I think you are trying to trick me!	*Damasō-to shiteru-no!* ♀ *Damasō-to shiterun-daro!* ♂
This can't be so expensive!	*Konna-ni takai-wake nai!* ♂♀ *Botterun-daro!* ♂

This is different from what I have heard!

Kiita hanashi-to chigau-wa! ♀
Kiita hanashi-to chigau-yo! ♂

If you think I don't know anything, you're wrong!

Damasarenai-wayo! ♀
Damasarenai-yo! *♂

* Change the *yo* to *zo* and the meaning becomes "It's no use for you to try and trick me. I'm not stupid!"

Don't think I'm stupid!

Baka-ni shinai-deyo! ♀
Baka-ni suruna-yo! ♂

Explain to me why!

Setsumei shite! ♀
Setsumei shite-kure! ♂

Think about it!

Kangaete-mite! *♀
Kangaete-mina! *♂

* While you're saying this, put your face closer to theirs, and with your index finger, touch your temple quickly. You don't have to do this, but it emphasizes what you're saying.

Don't you think you're wrong?

Jibun-de warui-to omo-wanai? ♂♀

Is this because I'm an American?

Amerika-jin dakara? ♂♀

I want to talk to the manager!

Manējā yon-deyo! ♀
Manējā yonde-kure-yo! ♂

I will never come here again!

Mō nido-to konai-wa! ♀
Mō nido-to konai-yo! ♂

I'll tell all my friends!

Tomodachi-ni iifurasu-wa! ♀
Tomadachi-ni iifurasu-zo! ♂

Hey! Tell me your name!   *Chotto namae oshiete-
                              yo! *♀
                             *Chotto namae oshiero-
                              yo! *♂*

    * To sound really cool, don't pronounce the first "o" in
chotto.

You better remember   *Oboete-nasai-yo!* ♀
   what you tried to do!   *Oboetero-yo!* ♂

CHITCHAT

Are you having a good time? — *Tanoshin-deru ?* *♂♀

* If someone says *Tanoshin-deru ?* to you, the best answer is *Uun* or *Māne* meaning "Yeah, I am."

You look like you're having a good time. — ◆ *Tanoshisō-dane.* ♂♀

Yeah, I'm having fun. — *Tanoshii-yo.* ♂♀

We're having a good time, aren't we? — *Tanoshii-nē ?* ♂♀

Did you two come here by yourselves? — *Futari-de kiteru-no ?* *♂♀

* If more than two people, replace *futari* with *san-nin* (three), *yo-nin* (four), etc.

Shall we drink together? — *Issho-ni nomanai ?* *♂♀

* "Shall we drink together?" doesn't quite make my top 100 list of all-time great pick-up lines; but nonetheless, it's very effective in Japan. If the mood is right and someone is eyeballing you, this is a good one to get the party going (or at least to sit at their table).

Has someone reserved this seat?	*Koko dare-ka yoyaku-zumi?* *♂♀

    * This is a cool way to say "May I sit here?"

Is someone sitting here?	*Koko dare-ka suwat-teru?* ♂♀
Do you want to sit down?	*Suwaranai?* ♂♀
May I sit down?	*Suwatte-mo ii?* ♂♀
Let me sit down.	*Suwarasete.* ♂♀
Scoot over.	*Tsumete.* ♂♀ *Chotto ii?* *♂♀

    * Literally means "Excuse me, okay?" You should point or look at the seat or they won't understand.

What's your name?	*Namae nante iu-no?* ♂♀
Guess what it is!	*Atete!* *♂♀ *Nanda!* *♂♀

    * You might often hear these if you ask a personal question. Either they're playing with you or they really don't want you to know.

What did you say?	*Nante itta-no?* ♂♀ *Nani?* ♂♀ *E?* ♂♀ *Nante ittan-dayo?* ♂

Where do you live?   *Doko-ni sunderu-no?* *♂♀

Where do you come from?   *Dokkara kita-no?* *♂♀

> * *Doko-ni sunderu-no?* should be used if you are introduced by someone. If there is no introduction, both *Doko-ni sunderu-no?* and *Dokkara kita-no?* are okay and both produce the same answer. Girls might tell you their address, or they might just say *achi* meaning "over there."

How old are you?   *Toshi ikutsu?* ♂♀

> * To this question, girls will definitely answer with *Atete!*, *Nanda!*, or *Ikutsu-ni mieru?* (How old do I look?).

Are you a student?	*Gakusei?* *♂♀

* The answer might be *daigakusei* (college student) or *senmon-gakko-no sēto* (student of a special school —i.e. dental assistant, cosmetologist, etc.).

What's your job?	*Shigoto nani shitenno?* ♂♀

How do you spend your time?	*Itsumo nani shitenno?* ♂♀
Do you come here often?	*Yoku koko kuru-no?* ♂♀
Have I seen you before?	*Mae-ni atta-koto aru?* ♂♀
Your English is good.	◆ *Eigo umai-ne.* ♂♀
What music do you like?	*Donna ongaku-ga suki?* ♂♀
Whose music do you like?	*Dare-no ongaku-ga suki?* ♂♀

Do you know this song?	*Kono uta shitteru?* ♂♀
I know.	*Shitteru.* ♂♀
I don't know.	*Shiranai.* ♂♀
Shall we dance?	*Odoranai?* ♂♀
Are you in the mood?	*Notteru?* ♂♀
Not really.	*Anmari.* ♂♀ *Betsu-ni.* ♂♀
I don't feel like dancing yet.	*Mada odoranai.* ♂♀
You're a good dancer.	*Odori umai-ne.* ♂♀
How do you know of this place?	*Nande koko shitten-no?* ♂♀

I heard from my friends.	*Tomodachi-ni kiita-no.* ♀ *Tomodachi-ni kiitan-da.* ♂
Where else do you go to dance?	*Hoka-ni donna disuko-ni iku-no?* ♂♀
How long have you been in Japan?	*Dono-gurai Nihon-ni iru-no?* ♂♀
Do you like Japanese girls (boys)?	*Nihon-no onnanoko (otokonoko) suki?* ♂♀

Let's party!	*Tanoshimō-yo!* ♂♀
Let's get drunk!	*Konya-wa nomō!* ♂♀ *Yopparaō!* ♂♀ *Moriagarō!* ♂♀
What are you drinking?	*Nani nonden-no?* ♂♀

Have you been drinking a lot?

Kanari nonderu? ♂♀

Well, drink some more!

Jā, motto nomeba! ♂♀

You need to drink more.

Nomi-ga tarinai. ♂♀

You're a strong drinker.

♦ *Osake nomu-no tsuyoi-ne.* ♂♀

Are you drunk?

Yotteru? ♂♀

Haven't you drunk too much?

Nomisugi-ja nai? ♂♀

Maybe you should stop drinking.

Mō nomu-no yame-tara. ♂♀

Are you okay?

Daijōbu? ♂♀
Heiki? ♂♀

You're kind.

♦ *Yasashii-ne.* ♂♀

What time did you come here?

Nanji-goro kita-no? ♂♀

What time is your curfew?	*Mongen nanji ?* ♂♀

What time are you leaving?	*Nanji-goro den-no ?* ♂♀
It depends.	◆ *Baai-ni yoru-ne.* ♂♀
If I have a good time, I'll stay.	*Tanoshi-kattara iru.* ♂♀
If this gets boring, I'll go (home).	*Tsumanna-kattara kaeru.* ♂♀
I'll help you to have a good time.	*Tanoshiku sasete-ageru.* ♂♀
What's next?	*Kono ato dō-suru-no ?* ♂♀

Have you decided?	*Kimatta?* ♂♀
I haven't decided yet.	*Mada kimetenai.* ♂♀
It's up to you.	*Makaseru-wa.* ♀ *Makaseru-yo.* ♂
Anything's fine.	*Nan-demo ii-wa.* ♀ *Nan-demo ii-yo.* ♂♀
Either will do.	*Dochi-demo ii-wa.* ♀ *Dochi-demo ii-yo.* ♂♀
I have a good idea.	*Ii kangae-ga aru.* ♂♀ *Ii koto kangaeta.* ♂♀
Good idea.	*Ii kangae.* ♂♀

You've got your head on straight today, haven't you?	*Kyō saeteru-nē?* ♂♀

I've got my head on straight today.	*Kyō saeteru.* ♂♀
This is boring!	*Omoshirokunai!* ♂♀ *Tsumannai!* *¹♀ *Tsumannē!* *²♂♀

* 1 and 2, if said slowly, are cool ways to say "What you said isn't funny!" or "Your joke is stupid!" They are also adjectives with certain nouns: *Tsumannai yatsu!* (You're boring! or He/She's boring!); *Tsumannē eiga.* (This is a boring movie.); etc.

Shall we leave?	*Denai?* ♂♀
Shall we go somewhere else?	*Dokka ikanai?* ♂♀
Can my friends come?	*Tomodachi-mo issho-de ii?* ♂♀
I'd like to stay here longer.	*Mada koko-ni itai.* ♂♀
Anywhere's okay.	*Doko-demo ii-wa.* ♀ *Doko-demo ii-yo.* ♂♀

I'll take you home.	*Okutte ku-wa.* ♀ *Okutte iku-yo.* ♂

How does that sound?	*Sore-de ii?* ♂♀ *Dō?* ♂♀
I wanna know more about you.	*Anata-no-koto motto shiritai.* ♀ *Kimi-no-koto motto shiritai.* ♂
Do you want to drink morning coffee to- gether?	*Issho-ni yoake-no kōhī nomanai?* *♂♀

* Old way to ask if you want to spend the night together (in bed, of course).

Our thinking is the same, isn't it?	*Ki-ga au-nē?* ♂♀
Shall we meet again?	*Mata aeru?* ♂♀

When can I see you next time?	*Kondo itsu aeru?* ♂♀
May I call you?	*Denwa shite-mo ii?* ♂♀
May I have your phone number?	*Denwa bangō oshiete-kureru?* ♂♀
Do you have something to write with?	*Kaku-mono motteru?* ♂♀
I enjoyed myself.	*Tanoshikatta.* ♂♀
Take care.	*Ki-o-tsukete-ne.* ♂♀
See you later.	*Jā mata-ne.* ♂♀ *Mata-ne.* ♂♀ *Jā ne.* ♂♀
See you tomorrow.	*Jā mata ashita-ne.* ♂♀ *Mata ashita-ne.* ♂♀ *Jā ashita-ne.* ♂♀

—ON THE PHONE—

Are you doing okay?	*Genki?* ♂♀ *Genki-de yatteru?* ♂♀
I've been doing okay.	*Genki-de yatteru.* ♂♀
What were you doing?	*Nani shiteta-no?* ♂♀

You're late.	◆ *Osoi-ne.* ♂♀
The line was busy.	*Hanashichū datta.* ♂♀
Who was on the phone?	*Dare-ga denwa tsukatte ta-no?* ♂♀
Hold on please.	*Chotto mattete.* ♂♀

I want to see you.	*Anata-ni aitai.* ♀ *Kimi-ni aitai.* ♂
I want to see you now.	*Ima-sugu aitai.* ♂♀
I'll call you again.	*Mata kakeru-ne.* ♂♀ *Mata denwa suru-ne.* ♂♀
I'll call tomorrow at six o'clock.	*Ashita rokuji-ni denwa suru-ne.* ♂♀

Please be home.   *Uchi-ni ite kudasai.* ♂♀

Say hello to Hisako   *Hisako-ni yoroshiku-*
    for me.   *ne.* ♂♀

—LONELY TIMES—

I'll miss you.   *Sabishikunaru-wa.* ♀
                           Anata-ga koishikunaru-
                               wa. ♀
                           Sabishikunaru-yo. ♂

I'll always think of you.   *Itsumo anata-o omotteru-*
                               wa. ♀
                           Itsumo kimi-o omotteru-
                               yo. ♂

I'll always love you.   *Itsumo aishiteru.* ♂♀

I'll write you a letter.   *Tegami kaku.* ♂♀

Will you write me a letter? *Tegami kureru?* ♂♀

I'll call you from Thailand.	*Tai-kara denwa suru.* ♂♀
I'll call you when I return.	*Kaette-kitara denwa suru.* ♂♀
I'll be back soon.	*Sugu kaette-kuru-wa.* ♀ *Sugu kaette-kuru-yo.* ♂
Please understand.	*Dōka wakatte.* ♂♀
I have to go because it's my job.	*Shigoto dakara ikana-kucha.* ♂♀
Take care of your health.	*Genki-dene.* ♂♀
Please wait for my return.	*Mattete-ne.* *♂♀

* You can use this anytime—i.e. when leaving your house, going to the restroom, getting a drink at the disco, etc.

Don't cry.	*Nakanai-de.* ♂♀
Wipe your tears.	*Namida-o fuite.* ♂♀
I can't stand it!	*Gaman dekinai-wa!* *♀ *Gaman dekinai-yo!* *♂ *Taerarenai-wa!* *♀ *Taerarenai-yo!* *♂

* All these phrases can be used for both sad and mad feelings.

It's difficult for me, too.	*Watashi-mo tsurai-no yo.* ♀
	Boku-mo tsurain-da. ♂

—EXPRESSIONS—

What a pity!	*Kawaisō!* ♂♀
Too bad.	*Okinodoku.* *♀
	◆ *Hidoi-ne.* *♀
	◆ *Hidoi-na.* *♂

* May be used in a sympathetic or sarcastic context, depending upon your tone of voice.

I hope so.	*Sō-dato ii-ne.* ♂♀
It's risky!	*Yabai!* ♂♀
Go for it!	*Ganbare!* *¹♂♀
	Ganbatte! *²♂♀

* 1. Used when speaking to no one in particular, such as rooting for your favorite ball team, cheering on the runners in a marathon, etc.
  2. Used when speaking to someone directly.

Cheer up!	*Genki dashite!* ♀ (b→g)
	Genki dase-yo! ♂

| Calm down! | *Ochitsuite!* ♂♀
Asenna-yo! ♂♀ |

| Never mind. | *Ki-ni shinai-de.* ♂♀
Ki-ni sunna-yo. ♂ |

| Cool. | *Shibui.* ♂♀
Kakkoii. *♂♀ |

* Said especially about boys and cars.

| Uncool. | *Dasai.* ♂♀ |

| Cool/tough. | *Moro-shibu.* ♂♀ |

| Awesome. | *Sugoi.* ♂♀
Sugē. ♂
Hampa-ja nai. ♂ |

| Cute. | *Kawaii.* ♂♀ |

Really cool.   *Saikō shibui.* ♂♀
           Sugoi shibui. ♂♀

Really cute.   *Saikō kawaii.* ♂♀
           Sugoi kawaii. ♂♀

Clever/smart.   ◆ *Atama-ga ii-ne.* ♂♀
           ◆ *Rikō-dane.* ♂♀

Copycat.   *Manekko.* ♂♀

Ugly.   *Kakko warui.* ♂♀
           Dasai. ♂♀

Weird/yucky (bad feeling).   *Kimochi warui.* ♂♀

LOVER'S LANGUAGE

10

I'm crazy about you.	*Anata-ni muchū-nano.* ♀ *Kimi-ni muchū-nanda.* ♂
I love you.	*Aishiteru.* ♂♀
I'm yours.	*Watashi-wa anata-no mono.* ♀ *Boku-wa kimi-no mono.* ♂
You're mine.	*Anata-wa watashi-no mono.* ♀ *Kimi-wa boku-no mono.* ♂
I want to know all about you.	*Anata-no-koto-ga subete shiritai.* ♀ *Kimi-no-koto-ga subete shiritai.* ♂
I'll tell you.	*Oshiete-ageru.* ♂♀
You look beautiful.	*Kirei-dayo.* (b→g)
You're attractive.	*Suteki-yo.* (g→b) *Suteki-dayo.* (b→g)

You're sexy!	*Iroppoi!* ♂♀
Look at me.	*Watashi-o mite.* ♀
	Boku-o mite. ♂
You have beautiful eyes.	*Kirei-na hitomi-dane.* ♂
You're quiet, aren't you?	*Otonashii-ne?* ♂♀
You smell sweet.	*Ii nioi.* ♂♀
May I kiss you?	*Kisu shite-mo ii?* ♂♀
Kiss me.	*Kisu shite.* ♂♀

Where?   *Doko-ni?* ♂♀

May I love you?   *Aishite-mo ii?** ♂♀

    * Two meanings: "May I make love to you?" and "May I
    give you my heart?"

Don't be shy.   *Hazukashi-garanai-*
                                         de. ♂♀ ·

Close your eyes.   *Me-o tojite.* ♂♀

I'm embarrassed.   *Hazukashii-wa.* ♀

You have a beautiful   *Kirei-na karada-dane.* ♂
    body.

Will you look the other   *Chotto achi muitete?* ♂♀
    way for a second?

Is this your first time?   *Hajimete?* ♂♀

Tell me the truth.   *Honto-no-koto itte.* ♂♀

Don't worry.   *Shimpai shinai-de.* ♂♀

It's gonna be okay.   *Daijōbu-yo.* ♀
                                         Daijōbu-dayo. ♂
                                         Heiki-dayo. ♂♀

Treat me kindly.   *Yasashiku shite-ne.* ♀

Is today safe for you?   *Kyō daijōbu-na hi?* ♂

I don't want to have a baby.

Aka-chan hoshikunai-no. ♀

Will you use protection?

Hinin shite? ♂♀

Are you on the Pill?

Piru nonderu? ♂

I want you.

Anata-ga hoshii. ♀
Kimi-ga hoshii. ♂

It's been a long time.

Hisashiburi. ♂♀

Love me more.

Motto aishite. ♂♀

More and more.	*Motto motto.* ♂♀
Do the same thing again.	*Mō ichido sō-shite.* ♂♀
How do you want me to do it?	*Donna-fū-ni shite hoshii?* ♂♀
I feel so good.	*Kimochi ii.* ♂♀ *Sugoku ii.* ♂♀
Touch me.	*Sawatte.* ♂♀
Bite me.	*Kande.* ♂♀
Stronger.	*Motto tsuyoku.* ♂♀
Softer.	*Motto yasashiku.* ♂♀
Faster.	*Motto hayaku.* ♂♀
Slower.	*Motto yukkuri.* ♂♀
Deeper.	*Motto fukaku.* ♂♀
I'm coming.	*Iku iku.* ♂♀ *Iki-sō-da.* ♂
Did you like (that)?	*Kini itta?* ♂♀
Did you come?	*Itta?* ♂♀
That was good.	*Yokatta-wa.* ♀ *Yokatta-yo.* ♂

That was wonderful.	*Suteki datta-wa.* ♀ *Suteki datta-yo.* ♂
I don't wanna leave you.	*Hanaretakunai.* ♂♀
I wanna stay with you forever.	*Zutto issho-ni itai.* ♂♀
Will you marry me?	*Kekkon shite-kureru?* ♂♀
One more time?	*Mō ikkai?* ♂♀

I don't want to get married yet.	*Mada kekkon shitaku-nai.* ♂♀
I don't want to get engaged yet.	*Mada konyaku shitaku-nai.* ♂♀
I don't want to think about marriage yet.	*Mada kekkon-nante kangaetakunai.* ♂♀

I love you but I can't marry you.	*Aishiteru-kedo kekkon-wa dekinai.* ♂♀
It's not time for me to get serious.	*Mada shinken-ni narita-kunai.* ♂♀

Don't get me wrong.	*Gokai shinai-de.* ♂♀
I need time to myself.	*Jibun-no jikan-ga hoshii-no.* ♀ *Jibun-no jikan-ga hoshiin-da.* ♂
I'm not good for you.	*Watashi-wa anata-ni fu-sawashikunai-wa.* ♀ *Boku-wa kimi-ni fusawa-shikunai-yo.* ♂
Forget about me.	*Watashi-no-koto wa-surete.* ♀ *Boku-no-koto wasure-te.* ♂

I'm sorry it didn't work out.	*Zannen-dakedo watashi-tachi awanakatta-noyo.* ♀ *Zannen-dakedo bokutachi awanakattan-dayo.* ♂
It's over.	*Mō owari-yo.* ♀ *Mō owari-da.* ♂
Don't be persistent.	*Shitsukoku shinai-de.* ♀ *Shitsukoku suruna-yo.* ♂

THE OTHER SIDE

11

I can't see you anymore.	*Mō aenai-wa.* ♀ *Mō aenai-yo.* ♂
I won't call you anymore.	*Mō denwa shinai.* ♂♀
I like you, but I don't love you anymore.	*Suki-dakedo aishite-nai.* ♂♀
I don't love you anymore.	*Mō aishitenai.* ♂♀
I have another girlfriend/ boyfriend.	*Hoka-ni koibito-ga deki-ta-no.* ♀ *Hoka-ni koibito-ga deki-ta.* ♂♀
I'm not interested in you anymore.	*Mō anata-ni kyōmi-ga nai-no.* ♀ *Mō kimi-ni kyōmi-ga nain-da.* ♂
Being with you is no fun.	*Issho-ni-ite-mo tano-shikunai.* ♂♀
You're boring!	*Anata tsumannai!* ♀ *Kimi tsumannē!* ♂

101

Stop bothering me!	*Jama shinai-deyo!* ♀ *Jama shinai-dekure!* ♂
You don't love me any- more, do you?	*Mō watashi-no-koto aishitenai-nonē?* ♀ *Mō boku-no-koto aishi- tenain-danē?* ♂

Do you have another girl- friend/boyfriend?	*Hoka-ni koibito-ga de- kita-no?* ♂♀
Please tell me. I want to know.	*Dōka oshiete. Shiritai- no.* ♀ *Dōka oshiete. Shiritain- da.* ♂
I'm sorry I haven't been a good girlfriend/boy- friend.	*Ii kanojo-ja nakute go- men-ne.* ♀ *Ii kareshi-ja nakute go- men-ne.* ♂

It's my fault.	*Watashi-no sei.* ♀
	Boku-no sei. ♂
Can't we start again?	*Mō ichido yarinaose-nai?* ♂♀
I'm serious about you.	*Anata-no-koto shinken-nano.* ♀
	Kimi-no-koto shinken-nanda. ♂
I can't live without you.	*Anata-nashi-ja ikirare-nai.* ♀
	Kimi-nashi-ja ikirare-nai. ♂
Please understand my feelings.	*Watashi-no kimochi wakatte.* ♀
	Boku-no kimochi wakatte. ♂
I will never forget you.	*Anata-no-koto wasure-nai.* ♀
	Kimi-no-koto wasure-nai. ♂
Thanks for the beautiful memories.	*Suteki-na omoide-o ari-gatō.* ♂♀
I'm so happy to have known you.	*Shiriaette yokatta.* ♂♀

Remember me some- times.	*Tokidoki watashi-no-koto* *omoidashite.* ♀ *Tokidoki boku-no-koto* *omoidashite.* ♂
Can we still be friends?	*Mada tomodachi-de* *irareru?* ♂♀
Be happy with her/him.	*Kanojo-to shiawase-ni-* *ne.* ♀ *Kare-to shiawase-nine.* ♂
I loved you.	*Aishiteta-wa.* ♀ *Aishiteta-yo.* ♂
I will always love you.	*Zutto anata-o omotteru.* ♀ *Zutto kimi-o omotteru.* ♂
I really don't love you anymore, so I'm going to change my phone number.	*Mō aishitenai-kara, den-* *wa bangō kaeru.* ♂♀
If you really love me, you'll stop asking me to eat sashimi.	*Honto-ni aishiteru-nara,* *"Sashimi taberu?"-tte* *kikanai-de.* ♂♀
By the way, how much does a Japanese wed- ding cost?	*Tokoro-de, Nihon-no kek-* *kon-shiki ikura-kakaru-* *no?* ♂♀
Forget it!	*Yameta!* ♂♀